© Roddy Lumsden

roddy lumsden is dead

ISBN 1-903110-00-84

Cover Design by Owen Benwell

**Published in 2001 by**
**Wrecking Ball Press**
**9 Westgate • North Cave • Brough • East Yorkshire • HU15 2NG**

**Roddy Lumsden**

roddy lumsden is dead

**Wrecking Ball Press**

# Acknowledgements

The author thanks the following publications and websites where some of these poems have appeared: *Dream State - The New Scottish Poets* (Polygon 1994), Dream State - *The New Scottish Poets* (Polygon new edition 2001), *Elsewhere Perhaps Later* (pamphlet 1995), ibid New Poets, Magma, Nerve (www.nerve.com), New Delta Review, *Oral* (Sceptre 1999), The Poetry Kit (www.poetrykit.org), Poetry Review, The Poetry Society website (www.poetrysoc.com), Poetry Scarborough, *The Reater, Rising, Snakeskin (www.snakeskin.org.uk), Such Strange Joy - Ten Years of Shore Poets* (iynx 2001), The Times Literary Supplement, Verse.


'Forecast' was commissioned by BBC Radio Scotland. 'Song (If it were only in a crowd...)' was set by the composer Joby Talbot for a forthcoming choral CD on Warners Classics. I wish to thank the British Council and the organisers for my involvement in the fifth Philippine-British Literary Conference, a trip which inspired parts of this book. Thanks to Caroline Barling and Jing Hidalgo who told me the stories about the carthorse and the goddess, respectively. Thanks to Nina Blackett for creating the Vitamin-P website and to all those kind people who have helped with this collection, all the members of the Lamb group and especially Julia Copus, Paul Farley, AB Jackson and Tim Turnbull. Lang may yer lum reek!

**Vitamin-P** - Roddy Lumsden on the web including contact information - www.vitamin-p.co.uk

*for my friends back in Edinburgh*
*and the Stoke Newington Contingent*

## Roddy Lumsden is Dead

# contents

## But Sweet

# Roddy Lumsden is Dead

(Altissimo!)

'Forget good deeds and great works, forget theorems and inventions. We ought to judge a man by how many women weep at his funeral.'

*Joseph Tournefort*

'When combined with guilt, depersonalization and derealization may be ominous symptoms because they enable the patient to take cold-blooded steps to destroy himself without normal awareness of the significance and consequences of what he does.'

*The Oxford Companion to the Mind*

'Stoke Newington is the place where terrorists behave like unpublished poets, and poets cultivate a justified paranoia.'

*Iain Sinclair: Lights Out for the Territory*

Edie:   Everyone round here is self-obsessed. Why is that?

Carr:   Well, it's because half of them are in love and half of them are in pain and they're trying to work out who's who.

*Elizabeth E. Montaña: Down Penny Alley*

# My Pain

*...one begins, ungratefully, to long for the contrasting tone of
some honest, unironic misery, confident that when it arrives
Roddy Lumsden will have the technical resources to handle it.*
                                        Neil Powell, TLS*

I'm trying to string together three words
which I hate more than I hate myself:
*gobsmacked, hubby* and... when I realise
that words no longer count for much at all.

And that's me back down, head on the floor.
It's like Cathal Coughlan goes in his song:
*I don't think I'll rise again
till I've seen how low I can go.*

It's like what my ancestor told me in a dream:
*You'll be a sponge for the pain of others.*
It's like what I told the lassie from the local paper:
*I do not suffer for my art, I just suffer.*

And face it, while we're at it, it's like
what curly Shona said that night at Graffiti
when all the gang were gathered for the show:
how she reckoned I would be the first to die,

or the time I slipped back from the bogs in Bo's
to hear my best friend tell a stranger girl
who'd been sweet in my company, *mind how you go
with Roddy, he's damaged goods, you know.*

# My Death

A woman's silver shoe remains sole-up
beneath a broken chair.  A china cup

with half an inch of something sour and green.
A thin, white line divides the TV screen.

Bouts of thunder shift the world all day.
A sweet voice says, *hold tight, it's time to pay.*

Millions quietly talk of their diseases.
The black-hubbed wind does as it pleases.

16

# My Funeral

Wrapped in *The Scotsman*,
the family hamster

in a Saxone shoe box
four feet under;

a suburban witch digging
in the mid of the winter

with a string-tied parcel
whose shape is familiar;

a dead-weight coffin
dropped into a merchant sea.

*Will I bury my mother?*
*Will my mother bury me?*

# My Post-mortem

Lost in the glue of an eyeball,
they find the natural darkness
which harried the top field
that night at Oldmeldrum.

In the pit of my gut, the surgeon
discovers why I kept so quiet
during the conversation on grace
in that restaurant in Jericho.

Faith remains in the form of a scar
halfway down my flank.
May '86 and October '89
lie undigested in my stomach.

Safe within my inner ear,
those three silent seconds
between 'Struggle for Pleasure'
and 'Gentlemen of Leisure'.

Laced in the boom of my blood
on an endless quest
is the salt of hopelessness
which confirms me as human.

# My Reptilian Existence

I feed just once a day, a swollen package
of cheap meat, cold veg, salty bread

and pungent sauces. I idle on the floor,
unable to move and consider my fate.

I taste the air on Manor Road for syrup pudding,
jail-bait, bin-fires, crack-laced Thai chicken.

I'd like to skulk along the railway track,
picking for kickshaws and tidbits

in the summerday greenery. You poets
can call me lazy, lazy all you like.

Why don't you hook my Scotch mouth
over your tumbler and milk me for my venom?

# My Fetch

One sunny evening on South Clerk Street,
I saw myself a hundred yards ahead
deep in conversation with some girl
and without reflection, I said aloud

*There's Roddy.* It was near the spot
where a few years before, I'd witnessed
a crone in a 1950s winter coat
flagging down a hearse she thought was a cab.

But tell me, does he justify my sins?
I might not be there to check his lust,
to bat his hand down when it goes for yours,
or when he slips his arm around your waist.

# My True Love

Here is the tale as it was told to me:
when the old cart-horse was retired,
the farmer's daughters rode him on weekends,
yet still, while plodding down the brae, they'd feel
him lean his great bulk back to compensate
the load no longer there: a phantom cart
which he was doomed to tow all of his days
as if a current buzzed uphill from foot to brow
and hot sparks dandered in his weary heart.
I want you then. I do not want you now.

# My Allegory

Mad as honey, jinking in and out of traffic
where Manor Road and Stamford Hill meet up,
a boy holds in front of him a broken slab
of mirror, walking blind while staring back.

It's a sure-fire metaphor for *something*, the very image
you'd spend a fortnight gasping for - an allegory
for the collapse of a community which once
left doors unlocked and meat pies cooling on sills.

Perhaps.  Or for the extinction of elaborate species,
the wayward progress of genetic engineering,
for the hotbed introspection of the artist,
for saints, fizzled to ciphers, who left us praying.

Or an allegory for the thoughts which swell my head
when you hold me in the lane behind the sweet shop.
That is, if metaphors for thoughts are still allowed
on this plundered and squandered nosebag of a planet.

# My Early Years

These last days in the back room at Manor Road
are plied with phantom scents: yesterday,
the air sharpened with the tang of sweet sherbet -
the stuff which was decanted, from a bottle
filled with gaudy drifts, into white paper pokes.
Today, it was the smell of pink bubble gum:
of Bubbly say, or sickly Bazooka Joe.
The main thing is, though others may know better,
I remember my boyhood as a happy time,
a silver time before the jolt of knowledge,
the shocks of ECT, the shock of love.
Look, there's Margaret, my childhood sweetheart
waving at me across two hedges. And here's
my best sand castle tilting its little flag at the tide.

# My First Crush

Everything can be neatly explained away
by something in our childhoods, so they say,

like Church Street down to King's X, one Saturday
a month or so ago, when one young lady

sat opposite me, swung up on the galley
seats - the spit of Milly Molly Mandy -

and bit her fingernails the whole long way.
That's it. That's all I feel the need to say.

# My Hormones

Does it begin with the still-warm waltzer seat
where fairground scientists detect
my Kirlian aura, a wraith wisp of candy-floss
and the outro to 'Ashes to Ashes'
by now only audible to a pack of dogs

who would blench and bay at the presence
of the White Lady pacing through the walls
of the ruined cathedral and would rather be
the Baron's harriers trailing through Tentsmuir,
bowling down that me-shaped abature?

Or is it in the moss and raindrop endocrinology
of the ninth hole of the East Bents putting green
which sits above the North Sea's stately nausea
as it washes through the boat-stones of the pier
where students parade in scarlet gowns:

these blunt blokes set on degrees in geography
and horsy girls from Roedean and Cheltenham
with their slang beauty, who, reaching the end,
can make the walk back, or jump on in? We poets
should keep our damned hands off each other.

# My Last Supper

A truck rams through the window of the café.
It's only there a second, but I see it
clear as a mirror, coming straight towards me,
my glass of milk, my plate of chicken curry,
my *Private Eye*. How painful that would be,
to be sucked into the innards of a lorry
and how easy it seemed earlier to tell you
I love you, at last, to toss it in among
our talk of crises we are living through
as if it was a line from some old song
*you*'ve never heard, but I have known forever.
The Turks chat as the radio chimes merrily;
the terror in the blue eyes of the driver,
the pocket money sleaze of R&B.

# My Dark Side

Just as my forebears, every winter,
moving farther north, grew paler
with a little extra fat marbling their flesh

and just as, after those two summers
I worked the beaches, I could only walk
as if the sand was thick beneath my feet,

so my women always sense a depth,
another side to me I hide from them,
behind the firewall, nurturing its luck.

# My Complex

Some of my classmates went to great lengths
to set it down in memory forever
that *chevaux* were horses but *cheveux* was hair:

Magic Marker flash cards held aloft
by patient parents, a school shirt cuff
with the rogue words traced in invisible ink,

while other kids were coldly unaware,
unplagued by doubt and kicked a tennis ball
repeatedly against the garage door.

Myself, I liked to think a proper training
in subtlety was something I could bear
and saw both sameness and the difference

even after Alison and I had paced
once around Kilrymont school in silence
before I asked her shyly to the pictures

*a week too late.* I knew then that simplicity
was what I had forever put behind me
as I watched her stepping back to class without me.

# My Water

The ox-bow lake where every creature
is the final generation of its species.
*The riverbottom where the proving's done.*
The dish-slops where the mince-grease sails,
blown by the whore's-blench of my breath.
The wishing well run dry. A mill wheel
rusted to whimsy. Prisms in the sluice.
The bath gone cold before you're into it.
*There's aye some water whaur the stirkie drouns.*
Atlantic meets Pacific. Streams of piss.
The days I wasted by the Maiden Rock
building dams where cold, cold water
tripped down from the farmer's fields,
to stop my life becoming all it is.

# My Limbo

It doesn't take the full-wind sickness,
just the mere, the constant threat of it,
just the salt trace, its faint knocking
to bring the spirits of chance and chaos
into this house - they stand in doorways:
quaint, foul allies, swivelling their ghost hips,
tugging at their gowns of transparency
and mischief. They buzz me with lust,
and I'm undone.
          Remember these: the Cupid
who ducked up from behind a wall and aimed
an arrow, one evening on Broughton Street;
whatever grabbed my shoulder at Earlshall;
a sound of heavy boxes pushed up and down
the empty hallway; the past is the self's ghoul.
What is it, Roddy, you know you've blocked out?
What left your brain so empty that it gushed full
with circus music and the safe bet of trivia?
Here I am swinging on the fence of fences, in limbo,
where the other world loves to try my pragmatism
and it's I who have invited them, summoned
by this self-indulgent ouija.
          But what is it
that folds my clothes as I sleep and leaves them
on the edge of the bed? Who hides my slippers,
re-hangs the paintings? *Déjà vu.* Did a minor
goddess filch me in Manila and follow me home,
prone, as they are, to easy-led mortal men.
And I'm easy, easy. So, come now, teach me
to believe in the soul. Hurt me with the truth. Press
me back down on this cheap, wine-coloured carpet;
let me know for once and for all how fucked I am.

30

# My Country

Supervised by Calvin and Zwingli,
two sour-mouthed wally-dugs on the mantelpiece,
Scotland is planted in her comfy chair,
knitting and knitting at something or other.
Her widow's weeds are nothing but the best.

She gnaws and chews and chews
and chews on a gristly mouthful of ethic
she can never quite bring herself to spit out.
Though to a man we agree she's awful bonny,
none of us are right sure what that means.

# My National Stigma

One winter's night in the Princess Louise,
when a brace of shaggy moths flew up
from the depths of my tartan wallet,
the Londoners said they felt ready at last
to ask me The Scottish Questions:
inevitable ones about the kilt, the work ethic,
the repression thing, our fabled gallon bellies.
And no, it wasn't true that we were mean -
hadn't I just stood a round of halves? -
that was just the silver-shy Aberdonians
and to them, just the Kittybrewster folk,
and to the folks of Kittybrewster, just Nan
and Jim Buchan in their bungalow, tugging
a stray penny between them, inventing wire.

# My Half-life

*I was aware of me myself in the exact middle of a living story,*
*and my body was my adventure and my name.*
*Dylan Thomas, The Peaches*

...but it was the phrase 'literally a goddess'
which took my ear, with its double-take logic,
its layers of fabulous imprecision, its position

just around the next bend in a moral maze -
how it made me realise my life is now half over,
bringing as it did pearls of memory: that first

and only time I undressed Cerys
or Becky on the tennis lawn at Earlshall
rehearsing that speech from *Lovers: Winners.*

# My Sex Life

*Come on everybody. Especially you girls.*

*Each day I think of something about dying.*
*Denise Riley, Shantung*

When those things happen
you thought would never happen
and they happen gently

on sweet-smelling beds in back rooms;
when you find a mouth
which completes the machine of yours -

two halves of a split penny reunited;
when you unbutton a body so perfect
and rounded it dips into the abstract;

when two girls invite you to cancel
the bed-space between them
and one is gun metal

and the other cherry red;
if you find you were wrong
in thinking your next sighting

of a naked teenager would be
an embarrassing confrontation
with a grown up daughter;

when such things occur,
there is something pulls us upwards,
farther than the hormonal rockets,

and that thing is the state of grace
from which, on my brief pyre of optimism,
I believe I will never recover.

# My Face Not Fitting

One night, way back in the Royal Oak,
two stranger girls were asked to guess
what it was I did for a living
or what it looked like I might do
for a living of sorts. And by and by
they came up with computer operator
and lawnmower repair man.
So it is I am among the number
of the Poets Who Do Not Look Like Poets:
you-know-who - the dominatrix in civvies;
Dreamgirl, with her county-set hostess looks
and that voice which could frenzy a stallion
and so-and-so with his ba'-heid, so
Irish looking that you expect to find him
untacking waffles of mud from boots
in the Shamrock Rovers dressing room
or topping and tailing turnips on Moore Street.

# My Old Flame

**0 documents found - 0.440 seconds search time**
which must mean one of three things:
the black possibility that you're lying
somewhere in pieces; the unlikelihood
that you've done nothing with your life
and are in a back room, admiring the view
of the wind combing a northern moor
or that there was some man beyond me
you were yet to meet, whose name you took
like a dear thing close to you.

# My Accent

Ask a Geordie to say *conjunctivitis*;
when in Hull, make them ask for *dry white wine.*
Ask a teuchter where Saskatchewan is -
he'll give himself away, time after time.

For me, *apricot scones* are in the *oven*
and don't expect much difference between
Patsy, singing 'Life's Railway to Heaven'
and the red-nosed joker in the circus ring.

# My Ascent

When dawn broke, I cast a little stone
into the mist ahead.  Back came a rock.

I put my plans together, sharpened sticks
and flipped them through the fog.  By nine o'clock,

I'd done the battle-axe, a steel harpoon
and by elevenses, the Gatling gun.

By four, I'd built a ship and reached the moon.

# My Descent

On a day like this, a palm placed
face down on the scalp
is enough to soften my skull.

One finger rested on the throat
will buckle the jaw
and I will speak no more.

Your hand pressed at my belly
drains my insides
of knowledge and order.

All this by way of healing me.
I must have faith in you,
for it's a long and wild way home.

I will feel my feathers fall,
my hard scales slough.
We'll crawl together to the sea.

# My Superstition

The toreador insect, the size and colour
of a brazil nut (unshelled) which I brought
all the way from Negros Occidental,
stowed away in my outsize hold-all,
now finds its way along the skirting-board
and begins to ascend the bookcase.
By way of entomancy, we will tell
what my life will make of me, but while
it climbs, there's time enough to roll-call
my superstitions: all those envelopes
I kissed for luck; the scissors I make
of my fingers to snip the invisible ropes
round my waist when I turn full circle;
the years of obsession with the number four.
The bug parades past Burnside, Copus,
bypasses *Brewer's, Chambers, Nil Nil*,
not yet noticing the volume on the floor
inside which it is fated to crawl and die
between the lines of the last paragraph
which describe how my childless ancestor
lay down, fixing to die, on a distant island,
his ear to the hard sand not yet hearing
the wet footfalls of the woman, peeling
and unpeeling through the shallows,
spoiling the silence of the moonlit cove.

## My Luck

They say I'm the head of a brutalist school
just because I've always known my place
and taken my chances.  The floor is strewn
with grapes and gooseberries where Fortune
has slipped and spilled the Cornucopia,
now just a filthy goat's horn hollowed out.
She lies concussed, her skirt about her thighs,
twitching the Rudder this way and that.

# My Theory

It was Sinéad who saw The Owl Man
hunched down in the vennel, feeding
the little cat from a can of condensed milk -
enough sugar to give it a stone-dead stroke,
though once I saw him, in the same alleyway,
hoist a can of Coke up to his mouth like a grail -
a *sacrifice* - in that feathery mop of hair-cum-hat.

Was it Fairbairn or Sutherland or RD Laing
or even myself who theorised that the mad
always have a physical affliction of some sort,
no matter how small - a witches' finger, a bung ear?
So please let me have just one summer
which I can call *that summer*, before these wounds
seal up, before my nose touches my chin.

# My Reflection

Late-night and bearded, framed in a mirror
as make-believe Rouault judge, white-faced and counting
his sins and his blessings - although I have neither -

I call myself sufferer, suitor, survivor,
repeating each, eitherwise deeming and doubting,
and switch between Budweiser, Silk Cut and cider.

The tiger feels no need to call himself Tiger.
He spends the night brassily whoring and hunting
and sees himself briefly at dawn in the river.

He paws at his rival, who ripples to nothing.

## My Sickness

A taint in the blood of my ancestry
(gracious, field-snug Chalmers blood),
a blind bend in the brain's maze
means that one of us is taken
from the back lines of the herd
from time to time.
                    Aunt Belle
was dragged down in the shallows of old age,
unexpected.  She sank fast and succumbed
before my first sickness had its full thirst.
In a late, lucid hour, she made acceptance:
*there's nothing they can do for me now,*
*but Roddy must be saved.*
                    I wasn't yet
inside the mouth of the whale
but I was fathoms under and couldn't hear
them screaming for me up above
and the bad salt taste of it is in me still.

44

# My Performance

Hélène Cixous, paralysed, blinks
and blinks through borrowed time
and the alphabet of her life story.

Billy Idol, raven haired and stocky
and preening at a tinny mic,
bawling out 'I'm Mandy, Fly Me'.

Jenny Saville chewing on a brush,
directing a spindly chorus line of fey
Elite girls, teetering on racer bikes.

And here's me discovering the price
*and* the cost of my performance piece:
*Roddy Lumsden - Char Siu Boy.*

# My Realm of the Senses

the liquoricy stink of badger dirt

a mouthful of pig's thinkers, chilled and raw

the cookie-dough complexion of the heart

that you need to be touched just there just so

the spitting sound of burning pigeon-wings

I know I know I shouldn't know such things

# My Life's Work

After an evening well spent attacking
a cheeseboard groaning with Cambozola,
Birchleydale bird's cheese and Dairsie Blue,
a Tupperware boxful of Triple-Choc Wishes
seen down with lemon sherbet tequila
and a seemly amount of your may-as-well kisses,
I jumped in my pit and got down to some dreaming:
*The Titanic thundered down Coventry Street;*
*a charm of goldfinches pitched into view*
*where a wasp gall ballooned on a Joshua tree*
*and then, in a bluster of premonition,*
*I saw* Such Things Occur, *my Selected*
*Poems, a pitiful pamphlet or two*
*and* A Living of Sorts, *a posthumous Collected,*
*privately published in a limited edition*
*by the sack-faced daughter I never knew.*

# My Meeting with the Goddess

You remember how, in the story,
the academic is shopping for socks
in a mall in Manila when the goddess
appears in the form of a shop assistant
who touches his beloved face and disappears.
My goddess decides to show herself
at a workshop in a sleepy Highland town.

She has chosen a champion disguise -
a restless German redhead, at least my age,
in a cardigan sewn with beads of rain
which shine there all weekend and never dry.
There's a new identity she's been devising
ever since she followed me back here
from the dark, sugar streets of Bacolod:

she's sweet but complicated, divorced,
a lapsed romantic wearing a cynic's hat,
with a wheat-free diet and six years
in the Findhorn Foundation behind her
(a nice cryptotheological touch that)
and a bachelorette pad over in Avoch
where she secretly whips up pans of *adobo*.

We escape to the firth-front to wolf
great platters of breaded seafood and salad,
to wrestle with tartare sauce sachets; our pasts
are shadowy, because she's a goddess
and because ECT wiped half of mine.
I recall something about a putting green;
she talks of a brief marriage in Switzerland.

I try her with *Unterhaltungsmöglichkeiten*
and *Selbstbedienungslebensmittelgeschäft*
and she laughs politely *(bahala na!)*,
batting them back with a Graf forehand.
Highland dogs cruise the streets; for once
I do not take the chance they afford
to move in close. I should have embraced

my goddess, should have held her hand
if only to feel it disappear in mine,
to see her shrink away, casting me adrift
in the back streets of a Black Isle town.
And weeks later, flying down to Galway
there she'll be again beside me: her thighs
broader and longer, the cute, tippy-toe walk

that screamed *Not German* gone, her nose
in a trashy Scottish novel (another nice touch),
but it *will* be her, biddable and tolerant her,
willing to deliver my baby-face, girl to girl
and town to town, in my time of sluttery.
For now, I leave her, dram in hand, at the bar,
talking to some local worthy, her accent

shifting from Negros to Bayern to Easter Ross
and tomorrow I will wake in the Japanese annexe:
my pomegranate mouth, my yak flank hair,
the skin of my back busy with mill-sweat,
feet beeling and dinging like buck-rabbits
and a dispirited girl will play a Chopin Nocturne
over and over, through in the sunlit lounge

as if someone had written a script.
Sorry: as if someone *hadn't* written a script.

# My Debt

In the all-but-silence, she breathes deeply;
I think of all the tears shed for the Lindbergh baby;
my debts like those of some small Third World nation;
My usual empathy with those who cut themselves
skews back-and-sideways into agitation
while, in her seasoned grip, I think of palominos
scorched and nodding in someone's 1930s,
breadcrumbs on a cream plate on a Dorset lawn;
the Mickey Mouse alarm-clock anecdote
which bears the bulk of my too-ready pain
and I can never spit it out.  My bedroom spins
as Harold Budd plays 'Children on the Hill'
and when she gasps, *just don't leave any marks,*
it's sweet to know she's thinking of him still.

# My Plea

Please once, at last, to be desired
for what I am not who I am.
To be loved for my stash of fire
and not my store of wonder.
I want love to be hollow, sham;
I long to be held under.

## My Prayer

For all the fools in loveless marriages,
for all the wretches stuck in dullard jobs,
for those in peril in the sea of faces
or stranded in the gyms or jails or pubs.

For all those under mental anaesthetic,
and those who're wrestling with the other self,
for all the dreamers starving in an attic,
and poor souls held at ransom by their health.

For those who live their lives in constant darkness,
for those who sold out years ago, please may
the emotional tourist in each one of us
cast anchor in a sun-spoilt bay.

# My Future

I think I know now what will happen:
Nature, after abhorring the vacuum,
will turn to me,
will stretch my body on a frame of urges -
*the bachelor wild at the foot of the bride.*

# My Solitude

Though we would wish to keep them with us,
we may need the beautiful to be with each other,
may feel it right and proper, in just the way
we cannot stop ourselves from finishing
a drawing of a face without the eyes.

Yesterday on the tube up to Chalk Farm,
to my left, there was a gorgeous woman
sitting with a chump and to my right
a square-cut guy with a kind face, so why
was he with that gawky puppet of a girl?

Some bilk; some take the wrong fork in the road,
but *fitness is the keystone of survival.*
And so I understand my solitude
and how this poem begins with my eavesdropping
a prediction of my early death

among my extended family of Edinburgh friends -
now sainted or broken or plain unchanged -
and ends here on Manor Road
by way of love songs, cognac and phantoms.
A few months single. Amicable. Mutual.

And lately, I find my affairs with women
freshly complex, keenly confusing -
the ex-loves, the half-loves, crushes, obsessions -
and I think of that old crowd, how I miss them,
looking out on the tracks here in cold North London.

Does it read like a draft for a suicide note?
For it's not that, never - not with the protection
of the other self (though *that* rogue might do it).
No, I've a coldness: a cool - not a cruel - streak,
the film star's full camouflage wardrobe, a soundtrack.

Here's a thumbed copy of *The Year's Afternoon*
by Douglas Dunn in the pocket of my car-coat.
Poor Douglas, out in his garden at Dairsie,
rocked dizzy by love in a way that I envy -
strangely - I, who must look through a glass

not darkly, but always, who can only focus
on one thing at one time with any fullness,
for whom grieving is just a vague stirring,
slipping as I do into my sickness
when danger starts up its solemn knocking.

And, sorry, I never do see it coming.
These days I find myself checking the window
of The Daniel Defoe and I know I am looking
for that girl - plump, fair-haired and twenty -
who sits there alone, composing poetry.

And what would it be like? Honest and plucky,
I reckon, wearing its flaws like hackles
on a cockerel and that is just as it should be.
*Make no apology for your apology.*
Quite soon in the script, that's what I say to her.

## My Pennyworth

So many are out there
saying the moon is beautiful
but not placing their hands
on the soft skin of its neck.
Know that, in your silence,
you have a sky in which
any hand might touch you.

# My Life

The fig was full of worms.
The joke was on me.
The joke went over my head.
I made myself hollow for others.
I took delight in the sight of a trap.
I learned to lie with grace.
I tried to hide horned animals in a sack.
I ate the food and then the food ate me.
And when at last I danced the music stopped.
The cream was skimmed too soon.
My wings and tail were plucked.
My mouth was primed with mud.
My larynx was a shrine.
I left the room to talk about the others.
The thorn in time extracts the thorn.
My years were two of yours.
No bird was of my feather.
I was blait and toom and fykesome.
The rice just wouldn't fluff.
I never lived it up
and never lived it down.
The fish was full of bones.
The skunk curled on my lap.
I was torn in the bush of ghosts.
The point was not worth proving:
the proof was in the pudding
in the form of a split penny.
The jellyfish was in my mouth.
The landslide happened in my mouth.
I pressed and pressed the button
but Truth wouldn't happen.
Time wasted me and I wasted time,
like the night lost in the wynds
and back lanes, searching for a strut
that will take my weight when the time is right.

# My Spring
*after March*

As some malingerer, a long time sick,
strives to force his raw-boned, bedsore body
up, one sunburst morning, muscles weak
and ribs ill-ricked, then so it is with Roddy
who wrestles with the memory of love
and who, despite his rumoured bag of brains,
can't pin the bastard, since no brawn remains
after the barb-strung malady of love.

58

# But Sweet

'Scrabbling in the depths of the bowl, he fished up an
alien presence, some slimy something that might once
have been an eraser head or a diseased Band-Aid.
"What hell is this?" he muttered. But he looked
delighted, slipped the relic into his shirt pocket, like a
trophy. 'My hobby," he explained. "I am collector of
farces."'

*Nik Cohn: The Heart of the World*


'Dim the lights, you can guess the rest.'

*Roxy Music: Love is the Drug*

# The Consolation

Though I hate to cheapen a poem
with slang, it needs to be said
that our brief time together
went *straight to video,*
though when it was shown at the Odeon
one hot night in Weston-Super-Mare,
by mistake, there was a standing ovation
while up in Redcar two misfit teenage girls
had seen it so often
you could see their mouths move in unison,
overdubbing our half-hearted sweet-talk
as they watched it for the sixty third time.

# The Lesser Spotted

All hail the minor Olympians:
Typhöeus who, with a hundred heads
still didn't nod his way into our thoughts;
Coeus who rode his twelve-oxen chariot
across the sky while Brewer was catnapping
and bold Eileithyia: what a story -
if only the teller could pronounce the name.

Consider the lesser works of art which refuse
to scream at us from museum walls,
which Collingwood and Gombrich never saw:
Manet's *Cricketers, Montargis,* executed
on a good day for cricket, but a bad day
for art; that sketch for Munch's *Melankoli*
where the sitter breaks into a silly smile.

Hail too those body parts which are rarely
spotted dallying on a centrefold.  Ten years
of marriage can pass before the cold afternoon
when sir leans from behind a newspaper
to say, *I long to kiss behind your knees*
and madam, arranging lilies, answers back
*Never have your heels looked quite so manly.*

# Weathergirl

In this horizontal, dim-lit world of bed, your feet
become redundant, though we might fit
curtain-rings onto your big toes, bonny girl,
and between them, run a string of drying hams.
There's just enough space in between your knees
for a stout school ruler, with which to measure
the lore of trees and the coming of summer.
But here's where only my tongue will go:
only my tongue and the electrical storm
drifting down from the north.  Miracle weather.

# Priapus

Year in, year out, I catch myself at it:
quelling the candle, drawing down the smalls
of the latest literary starlet,
crushing them into a soft, white ball

I launch into a corner. Deep in the carpet,
the dust mites, to whom I am God of Virility,
gaze upwards gladly at this cotton comet
which guarantees a season of fertility.

# Be Thankful for What You've Got

You're cooking - as you do - a pound of lamb
you minced yourself; you tweak a sprig or two
of rosemary, you add in mushroom soy,

a slew of Daddies Sauce, an Oxo cube
and then you spot it, stranded on the hob:
a centimetre scrap of meat, astray.

You curl your lip and dab at it, it sticks
there comically on your fingerpad;
you shake and flush it down the kitchen sink.

Within the week, an angry rash appears
around your throat which feels quite like a hand;
a sicky green tinge sleeks beneath your nails,

your hair comes out in armfuls and in town
the locals gasp and stare. The collie wails
and cowers when you set his food bowl down.

You notice that your tears are cold and waxy,
your nose is corked with butterscotchy phlegm,
the texture of your skin is natterjacks

and rubber bands. The surgeon's face is grim:
a gang of student doctors stony-faced
and shuffling as he reads the awful list:

inverted lips, spleen chasm, miner's lungs,
adrenal sulphur, yaws, vaginal teeth,
an acid bladder, white hair on the tongue

...the list goes on. You're strapped down to the bed
but, strange, you're thinking *such a lovely day
outside* and then *what shall I do for tea?*

just as you hear his droning voice say *dead.*

# The Misanthrope's Afternoon Walk
*(Southside, Edinburgh 1993)*

They're all out today.
The victims. The chipped on the shoulder.
The chivved on the cheek, the scarred.
Twinsets. Colonels. Lumps in leggings.
These mental cripples. Baby mothers,
repros, pit bulls, shrunken dummy-suckers,
Bad-moustached shouldn't-have-been fathers.
Some shithorse in a kilt. A braindeath
in a security cap. She who climbed the tree
of herself to take Eve's apple as a pessary.
Doctors with skinrash. Checkout girls
with threadworm. The sane. The sober.
Things that ought to crawl. Bleeders.
Greyhairs, pinkhairs, bluestockings.
The cheer-up-son recalcitrant I'd
dearly love to spine. Other things up
for overdue skinning. Ne'er-do-wells.
Existant traumas. Bed wetters. Kleptos.
Bores at the bar. Ratracers, boy racers.
The pierced, the tattooed, the body haired.
Those on necessary medication. Bored
mother, prammed sprog. The disarranged,
arranged married. Programmed. AAs.
TTs, TAs, SoBs. Clearance orphans.
Door openers. Little whistlers. Bo-grads.
Pick a cards. Toe rags. They're out.
Advocates. Recidivists. Low-rent fetches.
Twitchers, fornicators. Random attackers,
poisoners of baby food and cat killers.
They're all out. The ineffectual.
Mirror crackers, Sutcliffe faces. Showbiz
lookalikes. Household pimps, home breakers.
Tragic circumstance. The superstitious.
The witless camp who's down to the dregs
of his drag queen's resources. The other

resourceless many. The hang-at-the-door.
Pigeon fanciers. Narks. Original sinners.
Down and outers you might hammer
to a cross. Tell-tale-tits. Boozers.
They're out. Cathartics. Naebrains drying out.
Hangers over the fence. Natterers.
The victims. The challenged. The child bride.
The four 'O' grade cop who drags his sack
of drug-sucked hearts. Ten Regal Tams.
Carlins, bauchles and bodachies.
The hobbledehoy and the gran bene mort,
arm in withered arm. He who's always there
and will be, hand out, until he's washed
up in three black sacks. Termagants from
The Class of Nineteen Oatcake. Mousies,
cloppers, clumphers, the incompetent.
Mobsters, poor ones at that. Secretaries.
Bedroom centrefolders, drains, Little Nells,
spunkrags. Pale Sallys signing any scrap.
Hen-hearted primps. All hell's broiled family.
Fee-paying wantons. Daytime Valkyries.
They're out walking. Drastic short stories
you can't wait to reach the end of.

# The Great Northern

The cast of some future tragedy
is riffing through a cardboard box
filled with the dead bairn's toys;

the guttering spurts the best part
of a fortnight's rain.  A blue butterfly
wheezes to a full stop on a drain lid.

In Sabbath clothes, pinch-faced ladies
from the local Stoic Circle
mumble over sliders in Maria's.

And look, that's me (not Christ,
although it might as well be)
parading spritely, whistling a hymn.

# Forecast

The mist is lounging on the hill;
The smoke is loafing in the air;
The slothful clouds are standing still;
Dew slicks the nape-fur of the hare.

In monsooned Mull, it mizzles lazily;
The loch owns up two drookit dugs;
A permadrizzle pickles Paisley;
The corrievreckan gants and glugs.

The tramontana jilts the land;
The wet chinook bears icy rain;
The foul simoom runs rings on sand;
The santa ana scuffs the grain.

A white-heat-haze descends on Mali;
A warm front scunners Aberdeen;
Doldrums crack the cliffs of Bali;
Orchids droop in N16.

A force ten capers over Piper;
Blizzards vanish country roads;
A twister plucks a roadside diner;
Jack-knifed artics shed their loads.

The Yangtze-Kiang jinks and shudders;
The Amazon is acid rain;
The Nile's a smutty kid who blubbers;
The teeming Thames is England's drain.

Scattered showers feed the oceans;
The ghosts of Messrs Fahrenheit
And Celsius cry *"Rub on lotion,
Grab your brolly, wrap up tight!"*

## Higher Still

Then let this be our new curriculum:

the zooming-in of grainy flesh
on the lady dentist's drilling arm;

the oxymel of truth and sweetness
we spoon into our children's ears;

not shy first loves, but the chestnut tree
they sit beneath in proper songs;

not the chicaning of a mountain hare,
but the condor's shadow darkening its back.

# Seven Dials

A wide boy in a fast, white car
flipping through a wad of fifties.

A shabby makeshift shrine
to tragic knife attack boy Diego.

The ghost of the shade of the wraith
of a pub with a back-bar dog-pit.

Russ Conway's 'Side Saddle'
skipping from a third floor window.

# The Paradox

I take a conch shell, pink and chalky,
close to my ear and find the sound
of the sea braying and swithering.
When I hold a Coca Cola tin there,
I witness the same sighing argument
between sea-swell and shoreline.
Once, in the depths of the Underground,
I cupped a fat fist to my ear and caught
the casual swirl of the ocean's chaos.
Even in your performance of snoring
next to me, there is the fumble of some
beleaguered canal towards the Baltic,
the Amazon's anti-climax as it pouts
and gurns into the salty Atlantic.

# Drummond

If what you're asking me is *Am I truly sure*
*It was Drummond that I saw,* then let me say it here
And now that no one else has hair like fallow deer
And no one has a forehead like a vintage car,
Nor ears like skating rinks, nor eyes like Ecuador,
Nor teeth like wishing wells, that chin of chicken-wire,
The fortnight nose, a mouth like Milton Keynes on fire,
The smile he borrowed from a passing dinosaur.
For proof though, there's that little matter of the square
Root of minus one he has tattooed somewhere
We ought not mention and the halal abattoir
He smells of and that scrachle of a signature
Which adolescent girls yank up their boob-tubes for.
Believe me, reports of Drummond's death are gossamer.

# Easter Parade

Monday: herringbone cashmere blend ankle-length coat, charcoal cotton / elastane bodyshaper, sloe-blue bias cut camisole, loose-fit fleshtone funnel-neck sweater, sapphire silk-mix flat-front trousers, beaded fabric bar shoes in solferino red, fake zorino fur neckfiller and fingerless gloves.

Tuesday: alabaster scrunchie, INXS World Tour Official T-shirt, navy three-stripe woven sweat-pants, white Lycra bra top and bike shorts, peacock scoop socks, pearl and lilac padded collar two-lace trail trainers.

Wednesday: inside-zip platform high-leg boots in biscuit, mini-kilt with stag-skin sporran, heather mixture stretch V-neck jersey top, pomegranate plunge bra and tanga set with Swiss embroidery and boning effect, Missoni, printed microfibre clover casual jacket, wood-soot wool trilby.

Thursday: mulberry cropped mohair cardigan, shrimp stretch jacquard bustier with square neckline and invisible zip, cinnabar thong, pistachio crèpe palazzo trousers with velour trimmed waistband, burgundy ballerina shoes.

Friday: tar-black crushed fake-fur coat, dramatic longline cowl-neck fuchsia angora dress, siren-red satin balconette and briefs, kid-suede leopard print mules, dayglo pink pop-socks, Eternity, tangerine Alice band.

Saturday: logwood brown calf leather loafers with touch fastening straps, sheer midnight black pantyhose, fitted hobble bistre polyester pencil skirt with side-slits, hide-leather belt with Popeye motif buckle, walnut needle cord western style jerkin top, seamfree chocolate criss-cross bra and hi-cut lemon polka-dot tap pants.

Sunday: bunny rabbit motif winceyette pyjamas, The Crown of Thorns.

78

# The Cola Venus

After Pemberton's time of sweet alchemy,
the great fizzing vats of green stomach medicine,
saccharine, aspartame and phenylalamine
lurking like wallflowers in the wings of the lab,
the long day's drive of decaf for purists;
after *The Real Thing, Lipsmackin, Come Alive,*
*Thirst Knows No Season,* a glass jug rife with ice,
the aftertaste of nineteen metals on your tongue;
after cherry cola, that high-living, dandy cousin,
sickly gulps from the plastic bottle penny brands,
a conduit for white rum, bourbon, cratur blends,
the burst up and froth over of the Sodastream
whose syrup stains the Formica *forever and a day,*
Barr's Red Kola with its summerday bouquet
of soft sherbet, castor sugar and strawberry juice,
the protest march of the sued copycat brands:
Koca-Nola, Toca-Cola, Caro-Cola, Kola Nola,
the ester tang of Kola Kubes and Cola Bottles
and Fizz Bombs; after the superstore own-labels
which mothers glug out into ice-lolly moulds,
right where C on the map marks the secret recipé:
our picnic and the afternoon's keen heat, you,
head back, swigging, in that one piece bathing suit
blue, white and red, your mouth that hot, wet way.

## Pokémon

The first evening I arranged them
in the lounge window - the world's only cards
of Maghok, Molo, Rinobot and so on -
the neighbour's children came nosing,
their little mouths drooling,
their pupils the size of old pennies.

Next day, when word had got round,
a queue of quaking kids went snaking from my gate
right round to the boarded-up bakery. That thumping
is three small boys who're scrubbing down my attic.
That strange smell is a cross of Kate and Karen
cooking osso buco and Jason varnishing the hall.
And if Robert wants to go home with Rubachu,
he knows he'll have to keep his finger
in that hole in the drainpipe a few days longer.

# The Moths

A hole in the sleeve of a cardigan
no bigger than a penny;

what used to be a turtleneck
is now more of a V neck.

By the weekend, a brand new pair
of Oxford bags with a leg gone.

On Sunday morning, you wake to feel
your feet cold on floorboards.

By midnight, you're unpeeling bin-bags
to cobble together a makeshift tent.

# The Shortcut

On a summerday like this, you pay
for the delicious pleasure
of finding and taking a shortcut:

someone's little finger
will turn up in the heap
in the Used Tickets canister;

there will be the five wild faces
of the Matriani sisters
in the bay window of the bedlam;

news will reach you
of the death of a horse
you once rode across a burning field.

# The Six

*Give me his name and address,* I said eventually, tired of being mistaken for someone else, tired of hearing, *you're the spitting image...* And by and by, there were the six of us, peas from an outsize pod. The shopping trip was fun - six red and blue hooped polo shirts, six identical pairs of caramel coloured chinos, six pairs of Doc Martens cherry boots. We walked into The White Horse at ten minute intervals, never acknowledging the ones who'd gone before. This was going to be good, we knew, even before we discovered the Walton sextuplets playing dominoes in the snug.

# Song

If it were only in a crowd I'd lost you:
among the runners racing for a train,
the gangs of gleaners cutting through the pasture
at nightfall with their wagons full of corn
or in the swarm of suitors who surround you
or in the banks of clouds which bring the rain
which turns to torrents, rakes and swells the river.
For if I'd lost you thus, I might have found you
instead of knowing this - you're lost forever
and the actors who will play us not yet born.

# Song

I can no more be your fleece
    than fill the cup of longing
and since we have no gripping talk
    then grip is all our wooing
so slip one hand inside of mine
    and leave it there till morning
your left hand does not need to know
    what my right hand is doing

# Escher

Life spoils us with a choice of unfortunate combinations -
a dish of curried eggs, say, or being Italian Glaswegian
but nothing comes close to drunk sex in the early hours,

as I play your pale flanks with kisses, my breath sour
as I lap at the small of your back then dip up to whisper
*buttercup* at your ear, not yet knowing who you are:

a face on the dawn train or the girl in that print by Escher
who leans from her window and gazes down at the sky
while the townsfolk mind their business miles above her.

# Underground Literature

A gem of wisdom felt-tipped in a toilet
In an indie bar in Camden has you nodding
Your head in reverence, not realising
It's written there by some speed-snaggled student
Who appropriated it from an appalling
Vocalist, a self-styled Junkyard Poet
Who read the *bon mot* in a Henry Rollins
Import volume, and he in turn poached it
From some godawful manga comic book
Where it's spoken by a Shaolin grand-master
Whose face 'we' never see, or that the geek
Got it via Gibran from Zoroaster.
And that this chain of fools is never broken.
The whole bit's crazy. Everything is stolen.

## St Petula's Day

The smell of fresh ciabatta wafts across
from the kitchen window of The Vicarage.

The last red squirrel drops from branch to branch;
my wellies on a pile of Telegraphs.

As I stitch the second M of HOME SWEET HOME,
white butterflies beset the buddleia.

The neighbour is calmly strangling her husband,
England winning in the Second Test.

# Shibboleth

*(after Michael Donaghy)*

Ane didnae ken whit Oor Wullie's moose wis cried.
Anither couldnae slype the plastic
Aff a sodger's box ae twenty Regal.
Bi sic flumgummery we telt the fremmit-folk.

Bi the second week ae scrimmishin
We'd gone skeer-wud wi' friggle-fraggles.
At a sentry staund, in the deid ae a lashin-weet nicht,
Tae be toom-heidit aboot shinty wis gravaminous.

The morn ae the firsten peuchling, ah was ha'in a scrape,
Peerin intil a keekin-gless tacked tae a tree,
Rainin the gi'en names o' The Singing Kettle.
'Gary, Cilla, Artie.'

# Kingdom Jack Rubaiyat

*Jack Vettriano*

A grit-eyed laddie basking in the glare
of morning picture shows. The pitch and glaur
of sea-pits. This secret appetite.
A dancing master on a Kingdom shore.

*Jack Frost*

Having tracked the deer-slots through the ferns
and smelled the smoke-trails twining through the thorns,
the boy inside the man inside the boy
is guddling for the source code of the burn.

*Jackie Leven*

The Howe and why. The new toun mining stock.
The blues. The brown. The hands around the neck.
A cure, the core, the road. The fund of love.
The lightning voice in darkness. Long tale Jack.

## Naked

Believe me, it doesn't pay to dwell on
The Life and Death of John Holmes:
better instead to imagine a dark street
lined with willows, at the end of which
there is the lit window of an all-night bar
where sits a sulky girl with a glass of neat,
drawing on an Extra Mild and reading
and re-reading *Against Nature* - that,
or a hillside you stride over to discover
a sunlit field of ripe corn, where stands
a scarecrow in a raggedy Hepworth's suit
without which he is no more than a crucifix.

# One Thing I Do Know

...my death will not be natural,
there will be no heartstruck crumple,
no handfuls of gaudy capsules,
no redhead nurse, no chemo, no coma.

The blades of a helicopter will spin
my blood across a barley field;
a firing squad will pepper my chest
for someone else's sin.

Lightning will strike or a rare shark
yank me under.  May a little Turk,
whose nose I've just broken,
fix me to the wall with a meat knife.

That's the way to end a life
like mine.  May my wild eyed mother
count a dozen women at my grave,
their plump arms round each other.

# The Yates Children Burn Out

One was found with the first five chapters
of a novel hidden under the mattress
and a tear-stained diary entry claiming
poetry was no longer where it's at.

The youngest was spotted in a clearing
in woodland out past Stormy Corner
feeding a blazing bonfire from a bin-bag
stuffed with slim volumes and little mags.

They discovered the third one cowering
in the basement of Skelmersdale library,
gibbering, mad as fudge, which doctors
take as a certain sign he will write again.

# The Feyenoord Sticker

Somewhere (Ipswich?) was a cousin or an expert -
a kid with four of these things, unpeeled,
untradeable, fit only for idly flicking
at the raised eyebrow of a gameshow host.

However far out on a limb, we were rehearsed:
we knew there would be red and white, a proportion
of blonds, one or two sporting muttonchops,
three green goalies (more than any god might need).

Still the rectangle shone blank in all our albums.
Each pocket betrayed a brick of worthless swaps:
Honved, Malmo and the Greek one for which
none of us had the word.  Buggy Baxter taught

in Hepworth's beigery, was keen on the Vikings.
I looked up from Grace Darling or William Wilberforce
to see Gordon's face agape and frozen -
the missing stick insect standing guard on his shoulder.

## The Boy Poets

I watched one send a pair
of clockwork false teeth
waltzing in about the feet
of an audience of puritans.

The skinny, curly headed one
had a brand new Bag of Laughs
and could spark up a light bulb
with just his middle finger.

But it was the four-eyed boy
who unleashed the Smoking Monkey
with its little, cordite-scented
roll-ups who stole the show.

I was still doodling comedy eyes
on any word which had a double O.
My beaming mother egged me on.
I had a lot to learn and far to go.

# The Lost Boys

*'Many of the children who laughed along with (Kit Wright's 1980 book) Hot Dog would now have reached adulthood...' (Poetry Review v.90/4)*

Word leaked in that Willie Somerville
was midfield for United. One version
had him netting a hat-trick at Motherwell.

Josie Kirkpatrick was now a love goddess
and working for the Clydesdale. By her bed,
was a drawerful of massage-oil and love-eggs.

Even their old sport Chubby Chalmers
had apparently spawned twin podge toddlers
and was running the back bar at the Castle Arms.

After these twenty years in the book cupboard,
their little heads were thick with greasy hair;
their skin had the texture of butcher's paper.

Some morning, surely, a voice would break, one
would think of Miss Yates in a strange, new way.
Ears pressed to the back wall, they heard the fun

and games of nieces and nephews who hadn't yet
been born when last *they* saw the playground,
Pacman, Keith Chegwin interviewing Adam Ant.

Ten thousand games of hangman on the wall.
Even that great line about spam on page 12
of Kit Wright's *Hot Dog* had lost its appeal.

# Transhumance

These teachers - if not their charges,
then at least their mothers love them.
Oh and God does too. See how he causes
the afternoon sun to dip down
over the playing fields and settle

just there on the shiny trouser seat
of the classics mistress who keeps
the boys awake at night, how late light
glints there in the one soupy eye
of the tea-sipping Head of Chemistry.

Across the charted provinces
and parishes of rough books and jotters,
nothing has changed in decades:
a minefield of smudged graphite
laced with hot red ticks and crosses;

a hard-traced map of Great Britain,
lonely and baroque, while over the page,
year after year, they have drawn a herd
of grey beasts drifting back down
to the long days of summer pasture.

# The Wish

Yes, I think I would feel better
if they named a rose after me
or a far-flung star
in a seamless solar system,
if my thorns could snag
the fleshtone tights of a dithering gardener,
a teatime sky above her, the reek of hydrogen,
ten little planets swooning in their orbits.

## The Wager

Of three things you can be certain:
that four out of five will misspell
the word misspell, that the gravedigger
leaning on a frost-rotten fence
will be rolling a thin cigarette
and that, when at last you come,
I will still be this slow god
from the back of the class, yawning,
just getting around to naming things.

# The Divorce

...the two-bar fire, *The Fundaments of Chemistry,*
a travel shoecare set, the Arab Strap LP...
well, which is it to be?

The good egg, the big cheese, the old fruit,
when we divvy up the loot,
will help to fill the Volvo's boot.

Velcro, fusewire, Valentines,
Toilet Duck and turpentine.
Which is yours and what is mine?

The bags of bagwigs and perukes,
you're nuts I'm bolts you're eyes I'm hooks
since you got the brains I'm stuck with the looks

lips lap legs loin
the heart the hand the gut the groin,
toss a coin, toss a coin.

The burning bush, the golden calf,
each gurning, couply photograph
lies waiting to be torn in half.

Butterfly, dolphin, doggy paddle,
kiss and cuddle, Jimmy Riddle
slashed down the middle.

A Goofy Drinking Bird, the tickling stick,
your recipés, my rhetoric,
take your pick -
then pack. And don't look back.

# The Precious

I find myself privy to the following information:
it is not only on the pin-point of death
we leave behind the precious.

I trawl eyes-down through swarthy Ermita,
still hung-over from its red light days,
watching the pavement for signs of scuttling,

a creature bigger than that copper-tone cockroach
lying kicking on its back
three days ago and three feet away

from where I am writing this,
convinced there must be more
insectivora exotica in balmy Manila

than that poor, leggy waif
I whacked at as I'm now whacking myself
for not saying more to Merrilee,

for barely extending myself beyond
the international language
of stolen glances and longing stares.

# Simpatika

No one speaks more quietly than the lift girl
rising and descending in the library
at the University of Santo Tomas
whose whisper exists at one scintilla -
no more - above the effort of my silence,
whose words sound like tiny bubbles bursting.
Listen now - a stopped clock has more music,
a tray of water roars and rises higher
and yet when I lean in to choose a number,
I'm certain it is your name she is saying.

# Intramuros

She lies in her grand apartment
above the spick and span cathedral
in the heart of the walled village
above Manila Bay and she dreams
of the great, ruined cities of Europe:
Vienna crumbling into the ocean,
Warsaw in a plague of frogs and flies,
Lisbon, glimpsing in a fuzz of smoke
and London, where all the black men
have learned to talk like white men,
where all the white men have begun
to talk like these cartoon characters
warming their three-fingered hands
around a bonfire made of love letters.

# The Bastard's Morning Song

I want billiard-players to like me. I want clearstarchers to like me. I want quarry masters and turkey farmers and grooms to like me. I want corsairs and juvenile leads to like me. I want bagpipers and gem-cutters to like me. I want potboys and rectors to like me. I want gluemakers to like me. I want coxswains and cocklers and cowpokes and ostlers to like me. I want hucksters and tablemaids to like me. I want seedsmen to like me. I want sharpshooters and wet nurses to like me. I want the Little Sisters of the Poor to like me and the Little Daughters of the Rich. I want picadors and acrobats and valets and drapiers to like me. I want mystery customers to like me and gunmen and sexologists to like me. I want maltsters to like me. I want footpads and shopfitters to like me. I want bootblacks and gauchos to like me. I want oculists and miscellanarians to like me. I want sleuths and rubber-graders to like me and gleemen and buglers and sea-dogs and soil mechanics to like me. I want lime-burners and drysalters and lombards and higglers to like me. I want cosmonauts and the cast of Oklahoma! to like me. I want heirophants and brushmakers to like me. I want bargees and hogherds and the tinsmiths of Austria to like me. I want flax-wenches and crustaceologists to like me. I want minters and sextons and seminarists to like me. I want gondoliers and stagehands to like me. I want horse-knackers to like me. I want bluestockings and beefeaters to like me. I want finestillers and wainwrights to like me. Like hell I do.

# This Week's Releases

Watch as the last of the dodos circles
the symbol for ice an anorexic weather-girl
has hung in the sky, a full half mile
above the caber we call the North Pole.

*

Whether the morris dancers are Moorish men,
*morione* wearers or *morey's dauncing gentilmen*
or mates of Maurice who runs The World's End,
the maypole's still sick of the sight of them.

*

A sinking ship. The sea. A mutineer.
A desert island from a cartoon strip.
A sour wind whistles through the only tree -
a tune that's Number One year after year.

# The Drop of a Hat

After some months of indecision,
Sykes decided to do his dissertation
on those events which actually had
occurred 'at the drop of a hat'.

He came across a minor skirmish
in the Netherlands War of Independence
caused when a insubordinate colonel
tossed a general's cap in the mud

and then discovered the 400 yards hurdles
at the 1904 St Louis Olympics
was started with the drop of a beret
when the starting gun had stuttered

but that was pretty much the limit,
his paper was returned, marked 'without merit'
though Sykes was later to fall for and marry
a girl who appeared as if from nowhere

and bumped him squarely into the gutter
while chasing her bonnet down Market Street.

# Author's Note - Roddy Lumsden is Dead

A poet confessing to mental illness is like a weight-lifter admitting to muscles. My own periods of sickness - thankfully infrequent, far between and hopefully historical - were of a bipolar nature, combined with a textbook case of 'depersonalisation'. This fascinating condition, as exhilarating as it is distressing, is impossible to explain. Believe me, I've tried. It is sometimes described as being 'filmic', ie the sufferer feels himself to be a character in the film of his own life. Familiar surroundings can become unfamiliar. Emotions are heightened. There is a constant soundtrack playing and, as in autism, there is a delight in shapes, textures and patterns. Risk-taking, self-destructive behaviour and loss of inhibition are factors too. The earliest poems in the sequence *Roddy Lumsden is Dead* were written under the influence of this condition and the sequence is, in part, a report back from that strange, hilarious, delirious other side of the mirror, in an attempt to make some sense of that loss of identity and temporary death of selfhood.

**My Pain** - the song mentioned is 'Big Madness' from the Fatima Mansions' album, *Against Nature.*

**My Post-mortem** - the three seconds can be found on the collection *Close Cover* by the Belgian composer Wim Mertens.

**My Luck** - the goddess Fortuna is depicted carrying the Horn of Plenty and the Rudder of Fate.

**My Water** - the first italicised line is from the song 'yr mother called them farmhouses' from Robin Holcomb's eponymous debut LP. The second is a Scottish proverb (stirkie = bullock).

**My Old Flame** - 'ego-surfing' is researching yourself via an internet search engine. 'Ego-surfing by proxy' is to do the same for ex-lovers.

**My Theory** - the Owl Man is to be found crouching around Stoke Newington with his shopping trolley and matted mop which may be his hair or a hat of sorts.

**My Life** - this poem is inspired by material in *Ndebele Proverbs and Other Sayings* by J.N. Pelling (Mambo Press 1977).

**My Spring** - this is a version of a short poem by Ausiàs March, the 15th century Catalan warlord poet. The original is reproduced in *Sappho to Valery - Poems in Translation* by John F. Nims (Princeton UP 1971).

**Forecast** - the beginning of this poem is adapted from 'Self Communion' by Anne Brontë.

**Higher Still** - 'Higher Still' is the Newspeak name given to the rejigged 'Higher' school exams in Scotland.

**Shibboleth** - the original version of this poem can be found in Michael Donaghy's Selected Poems, *Dances Learned Last Night* (Picador 2000).

**Kingdom Jack Rubaiyat** - these quatrains are about three of my peers (painter, writer and musician respectively) who also came from working class backgrounds in the Kingdom of Fife.

**The Yates Children Burn Out** - the Yates family, of Lancashire, has had consistent success in poetry competitions in recent years.

**The Lost Boys** - a revered novelty plaything of the 1970s, the smoking monkey was a small metal monkey which blew smoke rings when supplied with tiny cigarettes.

**Simpatika** - the title is a Filipino word for a fascinating woman.